I am certain I will return to this book many times—to prevent music from becoming solely intellectual, friendship simply casual, and life experiences reduced to a progression of day-to-day events. Each chapter is a fresh and enlightening look at the power of music throughout time, and a moving glimpse into evoking the eternal power between friends.

Pamela J. Perry, D.M.A., Professor of Music, Central Connecticut State University

Kathleen Housley has written a sensitive account of friendship, courage, and the power of music to unite and heal. Her observations are sealed with a light touch of metaphors, never too much, always growing from the real experience.

Richard T. Lee, Ph.D., Professor Emeritus Philosophy, Trinity College, Hartford, Connecticut

Keys to the Kingdom is more than an inspirational story. It brilliantly connects neurology, music, language, and the overall sense of being. All rehabilitation specialists should read this book to appreciate the holistic nature of recovery and well-being.

Mary Purdy, Ph.D., Department of Communication Disorders, Southern Connecticut State University

KEYS TO THE KINGDOM

Kathleen L. Housley

WISING UP ANTHOLOGIES

www.universaltable.org

Double Lives, Reinvention & Those We Leave Behind
Love After 70
Families: The Frontline of Pluralism
Illness & Grace, Terror & Transformation

WISING UP PRESS COLLECTIVE

Only Beautiful & Other Stories
Kerry Langan

KEYS TO THE KINGDOM
REFLECTIONS ON MUSIC AND THE MIND

KATHLEEN L. HOUSLEY

Wising Up Press Collective
Wising Up Press
Decatur, Georgia

Wising Up Press
P.O. Box 2122
Decatur, GA 30031-2122
www.universaltable.org

Catalogue-in-Publication data is on file with the Library of Congress.
LCCN: 2010926564

Wising Up ISBN: 978-0-9827262-0-4

To Trina who has crossed every plateau.

TABLE OF CONTENTS

PRELUDE

A note at a time, a measure at a time. Haltingly, full of forgetting, remembering. One piano, two pianists, only two hands. Where are the sharps? The flats? Are they black or white? Locate them up and down the keyboard. Start. Stop. Which left-hand fingers can best play a right-hand arpeggio? Get tangled up. Take deep breaths. Adjust the arm sling. Begin again. Slowly the notes link. Become music.

So it has been for nine years, since Katrina Withey suffered a severe stroke following an accident on a snowy New England road. Trina (as she is called by family and friends) was a social worker as well as a gifted amateur pianist. The stroke deprived her of the ability to speak clearly and move easily, cutting her off from both her occupation and avocation. However, it did not cut her off from her love of music.

I visited Trina not long after she returned home from the hospital. It was April and she was sitting as silent and still as her grand piano. Yet over the course of my visit, she managed to convey to me a longing to play that was like magma, trapped beneath the surface and molten.

These brief reflections—some almost as complex as a Bach fugue, others as simple as a finger exercise on the C scale—

are about our odyssey to find a way to make music together. I use the word odyssey intentionally because in Homer's story it is not just a long trip; it is a difficult journey homeward, in which relationships play as great a part as miles logged.

A few reflections were drafted on the spur of the moment; others were written after much contemplation. Either way, my motivation was the same: to understand those times in our playing when disabilities disappeared in a shimmer of grace— times in which the composers, including Bach, Couperin, and Ravel, became present to us in their music. I also wrote the reflections in profound appreciation of the change in our relationship. At the beginning, Trina and I were merely casual acquaintances who shared a love of music and not much else. Now we play as close friends.

Physically, it has never been easy. When we started, I immediately became aware of several stroke-caused deficits (besides the obvious one of partial right-side paralysis) for which some kind of compensatory method had to be found if we were to continue. One of these is Trina's inability to move her eyes smoothly across the sheet music from left to right. Instead, her eyes tend to skip. The answer was for me to run a pencil eraser under her notes so she would not lose her place. Were anyone to observe us, she or he would find the process awkward: me sitting next to Trina at the very edge of the piano bench, playing with my right hand while reaching across the sheet music with the pencil in my left, but the result is a piece well played without interruption.

The violinist Pinchas Zukerman had a similar experience with his father, also a violinist, who had suffered a stroke. One day Zukerman placed the violin in his father's hand and then stood behind him. As his father brought the instrument to his shoulder and set his left fingers on the strings, Zukerman reached around to the right with the bow. Between the two of them, the sound of Mendelssohn's concerto filled the room to their mutual awe—an awe increased by the awareness that the weekly playing of the piece for a Nazi commandant had kept Zukerman's father from being murdered in a German concentration camp during World War II.

As Zukerman discovered, to dwell on the deficits caused by stroke is to miss the fact that what was essential about his father—what the neuroscientist Antonio Damasio calls the core self—had not been affected. However, he had lost the means of expression. To regain it, he needed the power of music. Unlike most rehabilitation therapy that tends to focus on one repetitive motion at a time or a particular set of skills, the *playing* of music requires a holistic physicality, an embodiment. When Trina and I play the piano, a myriad of different neurons fire simultaneously. As we perceive rhythm, cerebral energy spikes in our temporal cortices. For pitch, the neural networks in our frontal lobes begin to glow. The basal ganglia are busy getting our fingers ready to move smoothly over the keyboard. As we play, our brains are not only firing on the left or right sides, they are firing all over the place, even in the visual cortices. Everything is interacting in feedback loops of staggering complexity—all to get one finger to bear down on an ivory or ebony key, in turn to propel a tiny red felt hammer against a wire, making it vibrate into a single sound.

It seems absurd to point out the obvious, but music does not have space. It has time, and that means that music is reliant on the brain's ability to construct connections based on memory. A listener cannot identify a canon or a fugue if she is unable to recall the previously played melodic line. Nor can a musician keep the beat if he can't remember that the piece is written in 4/4 time. What is the result of this timely brainstorm? Simply the personal expression of beauty. As the composer Benjamin Britten wrote, "It is cruel you know, that music is so beautiful. It has the beauty of loneliness and of pain: of strength and of freedom. The beauty of disappointment and never-satisfied love. The cruel beauty of nature and the everlasting beauty of monotony."

There are numerous anecdotal success stories involving people who have suffered strokes. All hold out the hope that mountains can again be climbed, teaching careers resumed, and children hugged with both arms. One of the problems is that while there are similarities, strokes are as different as the people who experience them; the extent of their recovery depends as much on who they were as on the cellular damage sustained. The reason that Trina and Zukerman's father could return to playing music owes much to the knowledge and experience they possessed prior to their strokes and on which they were able to draw.

Not long ago it was thought that the adult brain did not have the capacity to change and that when damage occurred nothing could be done. Now we know that the brain possesses neural plasticity, which is the ability to restructure, reroute, and change the function of neurons in response to new experiences, including damage from a stroke. The brain's neural plasticity is sometimes described metaphorically as a bridge being out on the main route to a kingdom, requiring the traveler to map a new route using back roads. However, the playing of music leads not to the old kingdom, but a curious new one, strange yet familiar. Trina and I continue to explore that new terrain. These essays plot our amazement at the distance we have traveled.

I cannot end this introduction with the metaphors of odysseys, maps and kingdoms without attaching a caveat: Metaphors are inherently partial and flawed; therefore, they can be misleading. Similes retain the word "like" when a comparison is being made between two disparate things. Metaphors dispense with it; "the brain is like a computer" shortens to "the brain is a computer," wherein the comparison becomes the thing itself. The reason this is germane is because among neurologists one of the most prevalent metaphors is the brain as geography. There are roads and rivers, ranges and valleys, all of which can be mapped. And why not? Neurons *do* look like highways; the folds in the cerebrum *do* look like canyons and chasms; the various lobes are like provinces; the two hemispheres evoke an image of a divided kingdom. Unfortunately, that geographic metaphor can overwhelm other equally valid ways of conceptualizing the brain, resulting in a kind of perceptual blindness. The brain is far greater than a map and the connections are not linear. Toward such immensity, Emily Dickinson wrote: "The Brain – is wider than the Sky – / For – put them side by side – /The one the other will contain/ With ease – and You – beside – "

Trina is not a stroke *victim*, nor is she defined by neural plasticity. We do not play every week as a form of therapy. We are not practicing for a recital. On finishing a piece successfully, we do not affix a little gold star to the top of the page. All we do is sit side by side on the piano bench and make music together, enabled by the geographies of our brains that are indeed wider than the sky.

BACH AND THE BABY GRAND

For the *Prelude in C Minor* by Johann Sebastian Bach, I lend Trina my right hand and right foot. Her right hand lies useless in her lap, fingers curling around an orb of air as if a sorcerer's curse had partially worked, turning one half to warm stone. Her right foot is locked in a brace and cannot bend to the pedal. Even Trina's words are weighed down, strewn across a debris-field of language.

There are still times when Trina is too appalled by grief to play the baby grand with me. For months after her accident and subsequent stroke, she assiduously avoided the piano, despite its commanding presence in the living room. It was as if its wires were vibrating the word *lost*—lost career, lost friends, lost abilities—under its closed lid. Casting about for some way she could continue to make music, I brought Trina an autoharp so she could strum while I pressed down the chords. Together we sang simple folk songs learned in our childhood that rose up from deep and undamaged wells of memory, overflowing the silence of aphasia. Finally, the day came when the autoharp needed to be tuned and I asked her to play the notes on the piano for me, starting with the low F and ending three octaves higher with C. With great reluctance, she sat down on the bench and placed one finger gently on an ivory key as if touching the cheek of a comatose child. It was a beginning.

Now, a year later, it is early spring, though it is so cold and rainy outside it seems like winter. Alone in the warm house, we begin to play the *Prelude in C Minor* far more slowly than Bach intended but with great care, paying attention to fortissimo, pianissimo, diminuendo. The entire piece is one unresolved measure after another, the whole flowing like a rush of water, finding resolution only in the still pool of the last chord. It carries Trina along, allegro con moto, staccato on the third beat, giving her no place to rest, and buoying her up on the powerful notes of the bass clef. We let the metronome, which should be set at 120 beats per minute, sleep in its case; instead we synchronize our tempo to the slow drip of rain off the eaves, splattering onto the empty garden.

I wonder why Bach called this piece a prelude as if it led to something more. Perhaps he meant it to portend the future of young pianists for whom it was written. But for Trina, it is all she has—at least at this moment. We have tried to play the music of other composers (a simple piece by Beethoven took us weeks of struggle), but it is always Bach to whom we return. Some of his preludes are beginners' pieces worthy of a prodigy: fully formed; complex in their simplicity; mathematical but never formulaic. Their polyphonics provide the buoyancy of melody to Trina's left hand. Their counterpoint enables her fingers to answer mine. Within bounds, Bach's preludes are boundless.

Sometimes Trina suspects that I play with her solely out of sympathy. She does not accuse me of it with words, although she attempts to, but with a raised eyebrow or a sigh. Last year, before we switched from autoharp to piano, she tried to give me her baby grand, pointing to it and then to me repeatedly, almost desperately, until I understood and refused. The truth is that I love to play with her, not because we are any good or ever will be, but because we take the time to wonder at the music, to hear in the bass clef Bach's own sadness, to hear in the treble clef his joy. We do not wait for a miracle. Were one to come, she would play alone. For now, we play together, her left, my right, while Bach himself, like any good teacher, hums along.

SMALL TALK

On the way to speech therapy, Trina turns to me in the car and asks haltingly, "Why did you come?" The words are spaced out as if they are written on separate cue cards held up in slow motion by a prompter. I know she is not inquiring about my reasons for driving her to a cinder-block classroom at a local university on this hot, humid day.

"What do you mean?" I ask, aware of the intent of her question and stalling for time to shape an answer. She voices her question again exactly as before but with more insistence, even though her intonation remains flat: "Why did you come?" What she really wants to know is what motivated me to visit her the first time in the hospital following her stroke.

I think back to a late winter afternoon. Piles of dirty snow lined the city streets and the smell of exhaust from buses hung heavily in the air. Located on the edge of a poor neighborhood, the hospital used to be called Mt. Sinai after the sacred place where God spoke to the Israelites and etched the words of the Ten Commandments into stone. Now it had not only changed its name but its focus and faith, going from a full-service hospital to a rehabilitation center named St. Francis. It is said that St. Francis could understand the language of birds. I wondered if he could understand the language of stroke.

Not knowing the severity of her condition and uncertain if I would be able to see her at all, I had brought with me some poems, including Robert Frost's *Stopping by the Woods on a Snowy Evening*. I hoped Trina had learned it as a child and might be able to call up from memory the line "the woods are lovely, dark and deep, but I have promises to keep." Music and poetry are stored in a separate section of the brain, rather like a bank vault, hard to break into but not to break out of, because rhythm and rhyme serve as mnemonic keys. Indeed, Trina did know *Stopping by the Woods*, joining me on the only full phrase I would hear her speak flawlessly for at least another year: "and miles to go before I sleep, and miles to go before I sleep." Our reciting of the poem took the place of small talk about such things as the weather and the poor quality of hospital food.

For Trina, there would never be small talk again. All talk would be large, significant; all talk would be holy. Her question to me this day as we drive to therapy is holy because of the immense difficulty of its being asked, which explains my slowness in replying. A glib answer must never be given to such a question. To understand the difficulty, it is helpful to think of a stroke as a force-five tornado, hurling everything around so that after it has blown by, a chrome bumper might be found hanging in a cottonwood, a fork embedded by its prongs in one side of a barn, and the barn itself spread over three counties. Trina's four-word question to me ("why did you come"), spoken with the words in the right order, is a sanctified triumph of reassembly.

Behind her question is the fact that we had not been friends prior to her stroke, just acquaintances who were members of the same large suburban church. I stall with my answer because I do not want to give her the impression that I had visited her out of pity, motivated by a shallow compassion that would last only a few weeks before the chronic nature of her illness would wear me out or bore me, and I would go visit someone newly afflicted, bringing flowers or a noodle casserole.

"I always had the feeling that we could be friends," I begin, keeping my eyes on the road. "I liked you, from a distance: what you were involved in, your social work with children, you and your husband's commitment to Habitat for Humanity, even the way you dressed with a touch of art. But we were both too busy and our lives too full. We had no room for each other. Our friendship would not have happened." I glance over at her and realize she has begun to cry. "While I dearly wish the circumstances had been otherwise, I am glad that we have had this chance to become friends." I say no more. I just drive. She looks out the window.

When we arrive for speech therapy at the university, there are many others like her waiting in the hallway for the session to begin. Various word games are at the core of the therapy, requiring participants first to decipher the meaning of the question asked or statement made, and then to respond with the correct word or phrase. In this context, the word *games* seems cruelly absurd. These are not amusements, nor are these people playing for fun. They are instead stone lifters and boulder hurlers who are working so hard beads of sweat stand out on their foreheads. The effort it takes to heft a single correct word into place would make an Olympic heavyweight cry at the effort.

The first game in which Trina participates is a reenactment of a trial. Each person is assigned a character, such as the judge, the defendant, the lawyer, and the witness. They are given index cards on which are listed their parts and some background information. Though Trina cannot read her card without constant prompting from the therapist, everyone is patient, giving her time to sound out each word. More than once she runs through the entire alphabet aloud in a frantic search for a particular letter, stopping abruptly when it is reached to unshackle its sound. Then she hurries to link it to the other consonants and vowels she has already deciphered.

Too slow, she watches in desolation as the component parts slip irretrievably away, forcing her to start all over again. Trina's ability to recall lists, such as the letters of the alphabet or the notes of the musical scale, is common in people with aphasia; it is related to the fact that this sequential information was memorized rhythmically early in life. The problem for Trina right now is separating out the part from the whole, the single letter from the sequence of 26, and then maintaining its singularity.

Other people in the trial reenactment group not only can read the information on their cards but also can extemporize a little, adding factual details and emotional content, such as meeting the defendant at a restaurant prior to the crime, or using the correct intonation of a skeptical judge questioning one of the attorneys. Yet even the most fluent people speak hesitantly as if their words are wet bars of soap that can suddenly escape from their grasp to slide across the floor into an inaccessible dark corner.

In the second game, the group divides into pairs. Trina and her assigned partner work with a therapist in a tiny room accoutered with nothing but a little metal table and straight chairs set in front of a dark reflective window behind which unseen observers sit, including myself. Trina and the man who is her partner take turns describing a picture, such as an apple, printed on a concealed card. An exercise in categorization, it requires the person doing the describing to conceptualize the thing observed (the apple) and then to list its attributes (fruit, red, round, etc.). The second person must mentally bring coherence to the spoken attributes in order to guess correctly. For Trina, conceptualization and coherence are so brutally difficult that her body is stiff, her face strained, and her hands clenched.

In his book *The Man Who Mistook His Wife For a Hat*, the neurologist Oliver Sacks admits to his unease with the nature of much neurological therapy, concluding that it tends to focus on deficits instead of abilities, essentially driving patients "full-tilt upon their limitations." It would be presumptuous of me to conclude that all this speech therapy was for naught, especially in light of Trina's slow but steady improvement. Yet I can't help wondering what would happen if she were given percussion or singing lessons instead. What if she learned to paint, expressing herself in rose madder and burnt sienna? In light of our playing piano together, I am not being flippant. There is something draconian about Trina's speech therapy, which is based on the premise that if she is *forced* to seek for exact words, the words will eventually be found. So also in her physical therapy, if she is forced to do a repetitive motion with a robotic gadget equipped with springs and hinges, then new neural networks may be established in her brain that will eventually lead back to full use of the hand. But how many repetitions will it take? A thousand? A million?

One of the problems is that these approaches put the onus on the patients; if they are not improving, they are not working hard enough, they do not want it badly enough. I have been disturbed to see well-intentioned therapists, enthusiastic about new technologies and theories, unknowingly grind down desperate patients, including Trina.

Whether or not improvement is achieved, Trina pays a high personal price for therapy, running up an exorbitant energy debt that is never paid off, a debt increased by the medications she must take to control seizures and other medical problems. Exhaustion dogs Trina every day of her life and probably always will. Too often, therapists tend to view their stroke patients as if they were injured runners attempting to jog at sea level who need help overcoming a very bad sprain. It would be more accurate to think of them as injured runners attempting to jog at 20,000 feet carrying heavy packs, all of their red blood cells sobbing for oxygen.

After the session is over and we are standing in the hallway preparing to head home, Trina introduces me to a staff member, not using my name but a single noun, "friend," then adding after a long pause "for life." I feel a catch in my throat. As we head to the car, Frost's poem comes to mind, because Trina and I "have miles to go before we sleep and miles to go before we sleep." For life.

IN SEARCH OF ANSWERS

I am sitting in the middle of my bed surrounded by piles of books on aesthetics, the psychology of music, and the philosophy of language. There is a stack of recent scientific papers on mirror neurons, aphasia, stroke, and neural plasticity—that powerful two-word phrase on which so much of Trina's hopes are pinned. Balanced on top of the stack are two books by Antonio Damasio: *Looking for Spinoza: Joy, Sorrow and the Feeling Brain* and *The Feeling of What Happens: Body and Emotion in the Making of Consciousness*. The latter is a masterful presentation on the neuroscience of feelings and emotions and how the external world interacts with the internal world. Both books require and deserve slow, concentrated attention. My copies bristle with pink, yellow and green stick-on tabs.

I have been searching through all these books and papers to help me understand what is happening in Trina's brain. Thus far, I have encountered a range of ideas, many of them hotly contested. Certainly by "studying" Trina, bolstered by much reading and thinking, I will gain greater insights into how the brain works and the nature of music and language. However, Trina is neither part of a clinical study nor a laboratory animal. It is her struggle to maintain integrity that most impresses me. I am less interested in whether music is Platonist or neo-

Platonist, whether its mind-spring is hidden in the area of the brain known as Broca's or exists as a momentary tink in synaptic space. As the artist Barnett Newman summed it up, "aesthetics is for the artist like ornithology is for the birds."

Music does not carry information the way language does. That much is clear. Nor does it necessarily convey a certain emotion from the composer to the listener (sometimes referred to as the infection theory of musical transmission), even though that is a common assumption among music lovers. R. A. Sharpe points out in his book *Music and Humanism* that it is quite possible for a composer to write a funeral dirge while being in a relatively happy frame of mind. So also it is possible to write a love song without being in love. Many popular songwriters would be out of jobs if that were not so. Furthermore, emotions can be easily manipulated by music, such as martial music played at a rally, or a theme song for a movie romance. No doubt music stirs the emotions, but there are many variables. For example, a piece that moved me yesterday may fail to move me today depending not only on my frame of mind and physical state but on whether the performance is expressively overwrought or coldly technical.

This chain of thought leads me to discard another oft-expressed idea: that music somehow makes us better people, as if aesthetics and ethics were blood brothers. Anyone who hopes that music calls forth "the better angels of our nature" (to borrow Abraham Lincoln's words) need only call to mind Nazi officers listening rapturously to concerts performed by death camp musicians, among them Pinchas Zukerman's father.

In *The Aesthetics of Music,* Roger Scruton provides a different point of view about the power of music, which is that it shares with language the fact of inhabiting the human face and voice. "We hear music as we hear the voice: it is the very soul of another, a 'coming forth' of the individual. These descriptions may be metaphors, but they seem to be forced upon us, and invite us to treat the relation between music and language as something more than a passing accident."

Scruton's observation brings to mind Emily Dickinson, because in her poetry there is a similar "coming forth." To read her poems is to briefly inhabit her mind. I am surprised by the constant hunger of academicians to unearth more facts about Dickinson's life, for such knowledge is superfluous. Enigmatic Emily gave us something far better than an encyclopedic accounting of her days; she gave us broad vistas into herself. Yet the parallel between music and poetry is not perfect. Dickinson provides her readers with vibrant visual metaphors and a universe of images: bees, prairies, bells, snakes, robins, flies, windows, oceans. There are no such visual representations in a Bach prelude.

In the piles of books on music with which I am surrounded, sometimes the word *ineffable* is used to mean a quality that cannot be expressed in language. Each time I come across the word, I am reminded of medieval cartographers inking the phrase "here be dragons" on the margins of their maps, warning sailors of the unknown. Unfazed, I'll continue to read, but I doubt I will learn anything as important as what I already know: when Trina and I sit down to play piano, we feel humanity indwelling in the music, reliant on us to *body forth*. Nothing more. Nothing less. Ineffable.

FINDING THE WAY BACK

For the last half hour, we have been attempting to sight-read a new arrangement of the ancient Gaelic song *Be Thou My Vision*. The arrangement is plaintively beautiful, but with its odd tonality and its three key changes, it is proving difficult for Trina. It doesn't have the inner rationality of a Bach prelude. Furthermore, Trina's brain has misplaced the A note today, as absurd as that may seem. Every time the note shows up on the page, she plays either the G or B, the notes that bracket the A. She is annoyed because her ears tell her something is wrong even though her eyes cannot see it. The surgical precision of stroke has made the title of the song ironic. Fortunately, the loss of the A is not permanent. It has wandered off before. It is possible the phenomenon is caused by the medicine she is taking to help control seizures; or perhaps chronic tiredness made the A note disappear. Whatever the cause, there is no way of finding the A. It has to come back on its own, rather like a little lost dog that finally shows up on the doorstep, wagging its tail, unable to tell its owners where it has been for several days.

Trina has come very far since her stroke, continuing to improve well beyond the two-year mark when progress comes to a halt for many survivors. But today she is disheartened by the lost A. To encourage her, I tell her about the concert pianist Leon Fleisher who in the mid-1960's had to rebuild his career around left-hand music when his right hand began to lose its strength and his fourth and fifth fingers began to curl towards his palm. Known as focal dystonia, this neurological condition tends to afflict people, such as surgeons and musicians, who use small muscles repetitively and forcefully. In desperation, Fleisher tried everything, including aromatherapy, Zen Buddhism, and Botox injections—a treatment that has also benefited Trina, helping to unclench her hand. In large doses botulinum toxin (Botox) causes paralysis, even death, but in very small doses it relaxes muscles and helps control spasms. Unfortunately, the beneficial effect is not permanent, requiring the treatment to be repeated periodically. Even with the help of Botox, many years would pass before Fleisher was able to play—two-handed—the *Concerto in A Major* by Mozart with the Cleveland Orchestra. It is the best I can do for a good motivational story. However, Fleisher's cognitive abilities were never impaired, only his right hand, so my words of encouragement ring more than a little hollow.

I suggest we put *Be Thou My Vision* aside for another day and end with a Bach prelude. As usual, we play it in a way that gives new meaning to the musical term *grace note*. The word *grace* carries many definitions, including beautiful expression, holiness, and the favor of God. To me, the one that seems most appropriate is a brief folding of the hands in thanks—for the lost A note has found its way home.

LOST AND FOUND

The topic of the lost A note brings me to the subject of loss in general. I am neither idealistic enough nor Buddhist enough to be able to say that nothing is ever lost. Things are lost all the time; and not just things but also memories, abilities and ideas. I am not wise enough to determine what belongs in the irretrievably lost category, never to be found by anyone again. This afternoon is a case in point. Trina is too tired to play as a result of several hours of speech therapy this morning. So to pass the time, I have brought a very old piece of sheet music that I would like to try out on her piano, which is far superior in tone to my spinet. Titled *The Song of the Brook*, it is by a French composer named Theodore Lack about whom I know nothing except that he lived in the late nineteenth century.

I have never heard this piece of music before. It was among a raft of music that had been given to me by a relative who was an inveterate auction attendee. He was always searching for victrolas and old records stored for decades in attics, stashed in boxes on closet floors, or covered with moth-eaten blankets and shoved in the corner of storage sheds. Once on a whim, he placed the winning bid, all of four dollars, on a locked wooden box, not in great repair or with any intrinsic value. He was hopeful that it contained either wax cylinder recordings or tools. On opening it, he found to his disappointment that all it contained was music that had apparently been in the possession of a piano teacher in the 1920s and 30s. I was the only person in the family who played piano, so he gave it to me.

Who knows how the music came to be placed in that small box that was subsequently lost, only to turn up at an auction in rural Ohio among farm implements and furniture. I doubt that its owner willingly parted with it. Maybe he died or lost all his belongings in the Great Depression, the music among them. There is no way of knowing. But here I am, at least 70 years later, seated at a grand piano in Connecticut with the lost music, yellowed with age, opened on the stand. Conceived in the mind of a French composer, played then placed in a box by a piano teacher, purchased by a victrola-seeking uncle, and passed on to me, I play it now for Trina, who is too exhausted from her own searching for what has been lost to do anything but listen, perhaps to find.

NEVER LET THE MUSIC STOP

Today I brought the autoharp home, setting it on the top of my spinet and covering it with an old blue shawl. I had left it at Trina's house long after we had shifted to the piano on the off chance that we would play it again. However, it does not provide much of a musical challenge; plus there is the unsolvable necessity of two hands, one to press down the chord bar, the other to strum. If we stayed with the autoharp, Trina would never be free of me. With the piano, there is the possibility that she can play alone because there is an extensive repertoire of left-hand music, much of it commissioned by professional musicians who for various reasons lost the use of their right hands.

One of the most famous of the left-handers was Paul Wittgenstein, an Austrian pianist who lost his right arm while fighting in World War I. The Wittgensteins were an audaciously intelligent, wealthy, and distinguished family that counted among its close friends many composers and musicians, including Johannes Brahms (who gave piano lessons to the two eldest daughters), Gustav Mahler, and Clara Schumann. While all eight children were gifted, Paul and his brother Ludwig, who became one of the most influential philosophers of the twentieth century, were supremely so, not the least of their gifts being absolute pitch. Only Paul became a professional musician, but Ludwig, who played clarinet, never lost his interest in music. At one point in his *Philosophical Investigations*, Ludwig postulated that *understanding* a sentence is akin to understanding a theme in music, which led him to wonder about the meaning of sounds in music, which in turn led him to contemplate the meaning of *understanding*—essentially writing a kind of fugue, wherein the end loops back to the beginning.

Paul gave his first professional concert in Vienna in 1913 to favorable reviews, and all signs pointed to an illustrious career. Then the war broke out and he was drafted. In August 1914, at the beginning of combat in Poland, he was hit by a sniper's bullet and taken prisoner by the Russians. After his shattered arm was amputated in a primitive field hospital, he was sent to Siberia as a prisoner of war. Incredibly he survived, and in 1915, he was fortunate enough to be part of a Red Cross prisoner exchange. Determined to resume his concert career after the war, Paul began to arrange piano pieces so that he could play them with his left hand only. Then he commissioned music from several composers, among them Benjamin Britten, Richard Strauss, and Maurice Ravel, the latter's *Piano Concerto for the Left Hand* becoming one of Paul's favorites.

By dint of immense effort, he successfully returned to the concert stage in Europe, not as a one-armed war hero relying on the curiosity and sympathy of his audiences to succeed, but as a serious performer of a new, very challenging repertoire. Cruelly, his music was silenced a second time when the Nazis annexed Austria and determined that the Wittgensteins were Jewish. This was despite the fact that Paul's grandfather had converted to Christianity, his mother was a Roman Catholic, and his brother Ludwig had lived for a time in a monastery near Vienna. No longer allowed to give concerts and with his career again at a standstill, Paul immigrated to the United States in 1938, spending the rest of his life teaching and playing. There is yet one more heavy fact about the Wittgensteins: they had to struggle against the interior darkness of depression. Three of the five brothers committed suicide. Paul chose to live and to live fully. If Trina and I are ever in need of a role model, he is the one. He never let the music stop.

Never letting the music stop brings me back to the autoharp, now covered by the blue shawl. My grandmother played an autoharp, not strumming chords but playing full melodies written in a unique musical notation no longer used. When not being played, the autoharp sat on the desk in her parlor under a piece of black velvet that imbued it with the appealing aura of secrecy. Starting at about the age of six, I was allowed to play it as long as I was respectfully careful. As a shy child, I liked the autoharp because no one expected me to take lessons, practice, or play in recitals. After a cursory introduction by my grandmother, I was left alone to make music for my private pleasure, in the process learning how keys were constructed of three basic chords (tonic, dominant and subdominant), the centrality of triads, and the pathways winding between them. I discovered on my own that minor keys felt sad and major keys felt happy and that a song could be made more enigmatically beautiful when it occasionally digressed from its tonal center. I also discovered that straight strumming with a flat pick was boring but that by using finger picks I could float the melody on top of the chord. And I learned how to tune, turning each metal peg ever so slightly as I plucked the string repeatedly, paying rapt attention to pitch.

When I was a teenager, I saved up to purchase my own autoharp, choosing it from the various models pictured in the Sears Roebuck catalog—a black Oscar Schmidt with white bar buttons. Eventually I grew bored with it and turned to the guitar instead, teaching myself to play both folk and classical music when I was in college. My autoharp was put away.

In hindsight, I realize I owe that autoharp a great deal because it was the instrument on which I began and Trina re-began. Because of it, the music did not stop. As Trina looks forward to playing left-hand piano pieces, perhaps some commissioned by Paul Wittgenstein, I look backward to the autoharp with the kind of gratitude one feels towards a first teacher, long surpassed, who proffered you something precious, even though you didn't appreciate its worth at the time. So now the autoharp again waits in silence. Who knows for whom or when? I'll try to keep it tuned, just in case.

CREATING A WORLD

As long as a person can hear properly, music can find its way into the mind. However, it may not be recognized once it arrives, a condition known as amusia, which can transmogrify the most beautiful melody into the most monstrous drone. Fortunately, Trina does not have amusia, because if she did, playing the piano would be a kind of torture.

Music can also originate from within the mind, the equivalent of hearing voices. Such experiences can be uplifting or excruciating, the latter being the case when a song is repeated over and over. Fortunately, music is more likely to be palliative than deleterious. Probably the oldest account of music helping to alleviate suffering is that of King Saul in the Bible who found relief from his debilitating headaches in the playing of the lyre by a gifted young musician and warrior named David. Another example is the singing of Farinelli, a famous Italian castrato, who sang the same four arias every evening for ten years to the king of Spain, relieving (albeit temporarily) his suffocating melancholy.

In *The Man Who Mistook His Wife For a Hat*, Oliver Sacks describes an unusual case in which the patient, a professional musician, retained his musical skill while losing his ability to visually perceive the world as it actually was, including the identity of his wife and music students. Only by means of constant singing could he make it through the day, the melodies providing the essential power for the most basic of tasks, such as putting on a sock. If interrupted in his singing, he would be unable to continue, the sock dangling in his hand, an incomprehensible thing. Confounded by these strange symptoms, Sacks could offer him no help except for an unusual piece of advice, which was to make music not only the core of his life (as it always had been) but the totality.

In his book *Awakenings,* Sacks tells of the stunning effect of music on patients with Parkinsonism, unlocking them physically so that they could move again. One woman told him, "as I am unmusicked, I must be remusicked." Since those early days of neurological research, what is now known as melodic intonation therapy (MIT) has become the subject of intense study.

Just why music has such power is explored in a non-neurological theory put forth by Robert Jourdain in his book *Music, the Brain and Ecstasy: How Music Captures Our Imagination:* "Music's movement is more perfect than a body's. Physically, we fumble through a world of inelegant, discontinuous activity....But well-crafted music creates the very world it travels through, meeting every anticipation with a graceful resolution, and raising new anticipations at every turn." At the end of the book, Jourdain, who is himself a pianist and a composer, expands his theory about the power of music. To him, it surpasses mere beauty by enabling people to see the world as more orderly than it really is and themselves as larger than they are, providing a sense of transcendence, even ecstasy. "In this perfect world, our brains are able to piece together larger understandings than they can in the workaday external world, perceiving all-encompassing relations that go much deeper than those we find in ordinary experience."

Does that mean that people with amusia or simply with a tin ear are barred from Jourdain's kingdom of heaven?

That would be absurd. I think that what Jourdain is saying can be extended to all experiences that arise from a precise coming together of multiple elements in time and space, not just what is happening neurologically within the brain. For example, consider a sailor who, when the wind is blowing from the right direction and the sea sparkling, experiences an overwhelming sense of wholeness. Such a feeling can overcome a gardener kneeling appreciatively by a large peony, pondering the perfect coming together of rain, sunlight, and little black ants without whose assistance the bud would never have opened. It can overcome the members of a string quartet flawlessly performing together, even though just the day before one member had a bad cold and another was a beat slow on his entrances. And so it is for Trina and me. Often we don't get through an entire piece of music; a critic would certainly find fault with the quality of our playing; as for beauty, many pianists could with the most haphazard performance provide more. What matters to us is not the attainment of wholeness, goodness and beauty but the keen awareness that they exist.

HASTE, HASTE TO BRING HIM LAUD

It is late on a gray afternoon in early December. Trina is sitting at the piano with her back to me when I enter, her cane leaning against the right side, waiting, always waiting. A few weeks ago the grand was moved into the spacious living room, no longer banished to the dark ground floor only accessible by descending a long flight of stairs. At last it has found its way to the center of this condominium to which Trina and her husband, Mick, moved when their large house became too much to maintain and too difficult for her to navigate. The condo has solved some problems (no more lawns to mow, no more sidewalks to shovel) while creating new ones. For example, the sunken living room looked attractive to Mick and Trina when they visited the condominium with their realtor. Only after they moved in did they realize the extent of the challenge the steps presented. Obviously, the architects who designed the sunken living room were not thinking of people in wheelchairs or who use walkers and canes.

I hang my coat in the closet and rub my chilled hands together, then descend into the living room. For the past few weeks, we have been working on some left-hand music that Trina can play alone, in particular a piece titled *Klavierstuck* by Carl Philip Emanuel Bach, Johann Sebastian Bach's talented second son. Although C.P.E., as he is designated, was left-handed, he probably did not write the little piece for himself but as an exercise to strengthen the left hands of his students. The problem for Trina and me has nothing to do with difficulty; the problem is that the notes are too small and are printed too close together on the sheet music, making it difficult for Trina to visually keep her place. My trick of running the eraser end of a yellow Ticonderoga pencil under her notes is not working because the eraser is underscoring at least two notes at a time. I think that I may have to copy *Klavierstuck* by hand, making the notes larger and blacker with more white space.

Because of the problem with the left-hand music, Trina has decided to play Christmas carols today. "I don't know, but we try," she says firmly. I sit down beside her on the bench and she begins to sight-read the bass clef notes. Then abruptly, she signals to me to trade places with her on the bench (with me sitting to her left instead of to her right), because she wants to attempt to play the melody. This is much more arduous for her because her left hand must decipher the position of the notes in the treble clef. While it is true that memory and melody reside in the brain, they also reside in the bend of the fingers, the muscles of the hands, the angle of the arms, even the slope of the back. Rarely does the left hand ascend from the bass into the treble, which is why Trina's left hand does not know as thoroughly the things that her right hand knows but can no longer express.

When she starts to get frustrated, I suggest we sing the melodies instead of playing them. She chooses *What Child Is This?* And so we begin to sing a medieval carol in a minor key as the cold light thins outside the window and the leafless woods beyond the little yard fill with darkness. We don't sound very good; her notes are wobbly. However, she gets all the words right except where some well-meaning but misguided editor has modernized the last line, substituting "come come to bring him praise" for the standard wording "haste haste to bring him laud," probably judging it to be antiquated. Because I am reading the words, I sing it the new way, but Trina, who is relying on memory, sings it the old way and immediately fumbles. I tell her that the old words are hard-wired in her brain and to stick with them. Furthermore, I like the image they evoke of hurrying through the winter night to praise.

As I head home through light snow that has just begun to fall, it occurs to me that *laud* is a fine word. So also *haste*. For Trina, they combine into an eloquence that cannot be spoken, only sung.

THE PATIENCE OF SAINTS

The first reflection in this collection was written on Tuesday May 14, 2002, a year after Trina and I shifted from autoharp to piano. I have the date memorized because on the following day, Wednesday May 15, my 84-year-old mother, who lived with my husband and me, had a serious stroke.

The idea for *Bach and the Baby Grand* had been in my mind for a month, but I had not done much about it until I woke that Tuesday morning with a sense of urgency. I had the feeling that if I did not write it immediately it would never be written. The feeling was so strong, I complied. Many months would pass before I would write again. During that time, I came to know the meaning of patience. Like Trina, my mother is a kind, caring person who prior to her stroke had always worked very hard and had never been a burden to anyone. Suddenly she was unable to walk alone, to speak understandably, or to see clearly. She felt vulnerable, helpless and hopeless. Slowly my mother improved to the point that she was able to move to a nearby assisted living community. The arrangement worked out very well and she was content there until another stroke made the move to a nursing home necessary.

Many wonderful books have been written by or about people who have serious health problems or who are dying.

Most recommend valuing the present moment, taking the time to contemplate things such as the beauty of the snowflake or the laughter of a child. No doubt these books are important; in fact, I own a few that I make a point of rereading when I find myself losing the ability to focus on what matters in life. However, I think the writers of these books would be more truthful if they included the thoughts and emotions not only of the wise patients but also of the harried caregivers who are faced with mounting loses in their own lives. While I was caring for my mother, I would have loved to have had the time to contemplate snowflakes, but I was too busy trying to meet her most basic needs, including getting her into and out of the bathroom and cleaning up accidents. Were I to have found the time to sit down and think about the laughter of a child, chances are I would have in the same instant realized that my mother was running short of a critical medicine, necessitating a dash to the drugstore before it closed—a dash made more difficult by her extreme anxiety in my absence even though someone was always with her. Yet when friends and family stopped by to visit, they found her well dressed and smiling, at ease in her blue chair before the window. They rarely had any idea of the amount of work and patience that had gone into achieving that semblance of equanimity.

Because of my experience with my mother, when I look at Trina's husband Mick folding the laundry into neat piles on the dining room table before heading out to go food shopping, it is with a sense of profound respect for the complexity of his life. While Trina is the one who sits beside me on the piano bench, Mick is the one who helped get her there.

Even saints, those paragons of virtue, would rather not have to be patient. It is the only virtue connected to the flow of time and our own assessment of how quickly things should be progressing. It also is affected by the severity of the possible outcome. If everything and everyone is flowing along at a normal rate, for example, a project is progressing smoothly or a plane arrives on time, then patience is not needed. But if something or someone impedes the flow, impatience rears up like a standing wave.

For Trina, it takes patience when the words won't come. It takes even more patience to put up with people who misunderstand or who don't allow her enough time. Such was the case earlier today when I drove Trina to another speech therapy session. I watched through the one-way glass window as she took part in a conversation group. The goal was for the participants to carry on a sustained conversation in which they took turns talking about a topic of personal interest. Trina led off with a hesitant description of her recent trip to France during which she and Mick traveled by barge on the canals and rivers, touring castles and wineries along the way. Trina used the words "barge" and "river" correctly, but the young therapist kept correcting her, substituting "ship" and "ocean" as if they had taken a cruise on the Mediterranean. Trina took the inappropriate corrections and interruptions in stride. I was the one who became impatient, saying to myself, "No, no, she's right, let her continue." After class on our way home, I reassured Trina that she had done an admirable job. I suggested she bring in photos of the trip the following week to show the therapist that *barge* and *river* were correct.

Playing the piano also takes great patience on Trina's part, as does waiting for me to arrive so as to play a piece totally. I have often walked into her living room to find her practicing half an arpeggio or part of a chord. The feeling is of famished sound. This is why I would like her to learn to play music written for the left hand only. However, she has been reluctant to do so, perhaps because she sees it as capitulation. Trina is still hopeful about regaining the use of her right hand. Because hope is, as Dickinson described it, "the thing with feathers/that perches in the soul/And sings the tune without the words," it is crucial that I uphold it for Trina. And that requires me to be patient as well.

THE BLUE MITTENS

It is frigid with the temperature in the low teens and a stiff breeze that swirls the dry snow into little white whirlwinds. This afternoon, Trina and I are going to attend a performance of a boys' choir. Getting ready to head out into the cold, she removes the sling and maneuvers her right arm carefully into the sleeve of her coat. But a problem arises when she comes to the gloves. She is unable to pull one onto her paralyzed right hand, and she does not know where her mittens are. As we walk to the car from the house, navigating carefully around patches of ice, I place my gloved left hand over her right to keep it warm. Her fingers hurt if any pressure is applied, so I do it gently, as if I were trapping a small curled-up animal under my cupped hand.

Having dropped Trina off after the concert, I am back home rifling through the box on the floor of my disorganized kitchen closet in search of mittens that once belonged to my sons, now grown men. And there they are: knit in a variegated blue yarn by my mother. Not only are the mittens the right size and in good shape but they are soft and stretchy, which will enable Trina to thrust in her fist without worrying about uncurling the fingers or placing the thumb correctly.

ॐ

A few days have gone by and I am at Trina's again with the blue mittens stuffed in my coat pocket. Trina beams when I pull them out. Not only do they fit, but also they are the right shade of blue to match her coat. It would be tempting to conclude that those mittens have been waiting for this moment; that for too many years to reckon, God has prevented me from throwing them out or giving them away. However, if God were providential enough to save mittens for a cold day in January, God could have been providential enough to prevent stroke. I will not get theologically maudlin about mittens. Yet I am of a mind to give thanks when something small or large, important or unimportant, fills a need. Mittens or music—it makes no difference, the point is to be grateful for what is right and good.

Today we play a simple rondo by François Couperin. Rondos, with their recurring themes, are always excellent for us because if we don't get the notes right the first time we will have several more chances. This one is a little pleasure, circling back on itself playfully, as light as a spring zephyr. Couperin was a child prodigy who was born in 1668, 17 years before Bach. He began to play the organ at St. Gervais in Paris when he was only ten after the untimely death of his father who had been the organist. I can imagine him as a little boy walking across the stone floor on his way to practice the organ. His light lonely footfall echoes in the vast empty space. Cathedrals are cold, drafty places in the wintertime. To keep his hands warm, he wears a pair of blue mittens.

THE DANGLING MODIFIER

Another year has gone by and in a few days it will be Christmas again. However, this year the holiday will be different because Trina and Mick have just moved from the old condominium with the impossible sunken living room to a new condominium that is on one floor. There are no more stairs for her to climb with a braced leg. From the outside, it resembles a modest 1920's bungalow painted gray with a red door and a small front porch enclosed by a white railing. But inside it bears no resemblance to the dark, cramped domestic interiors of the Jazz Age. It is spacious and airy with a vaulted ceiling in the great room and many south-facing windows flooding it with light.

It is one of the first stand-alone units to be built in a new development that I trust will be very nice—eventually. At the moment, the little house sits forlornly in a sea of congealed mud amidst a half-submerged archipelago of boulders, each rimmed by thin sheets of cracked ice. The air is filled with the rumble of bulldozers digging cellar holes, the snarl of power saws, and the pneumatic pop of nail-guns. A fresh concealing layer of pure white snow would be most appreciated, but it has been warm, wet, and dismal in New England.

Inside there are no curtains on the windows; then

again there are no neighbors either. Pictures lean against walls, furniture is haphazardly arranged, and boxes are piled on boxes. The piano music is packed in one of them. A poinsettia, the solitary sign of the season, stands at the end of a cluttered horizontal surface that I take on faith to be the dining room table.

Impervious to the clutter, the grand piano resides in its own spacious corner. In the living room of the former condo, the sofa had to be moved down to the basement to make room for the piano; there was not enough space for both. Here that is not a problem. And without neighbors on the other side of the wall, there is no reason not to raise the lid all the way up.

After moving the music rack into bifocal range, getting down on my knees to plug in the brass piano lamp (struggling to find an electrical outlet that works), and finally adjusting the position of the bench, I sit down and begin to play Tchaikovsky's *June* from *The Seasons* as a kind of house-warming gift to Trina. This is a dangerous gift albeit one she has requested. I don't often play solo for her because it is too much of a reminder of what she could once do better than I. When we play together, we are working on the possible-present, not the impossible-once-was. But when I play by myself, there floats into the room a solemn beauty. Amplified by loss, it is similar to the exquisiteness of a lone surviving child whose presence can't help but conjure absence. While I play, Trina turns her head away.

Trina asked me to play *June* a few weeks ago, but I declined because I am not a proficient sight-reader and I didn't want to mangle it. Instead, I borrowed the well-marked-up music (including the date on which she first played it and the name of her teacher) and have spent a fair amount of time practicing, trying to determine if there were a way we could play it together. Unfortunately, I concluded that there wasn't, the principal problem being that the piece changes key abruptly. Trina can play any key in which we begin, provided it doesn't have more than three sharps or flats, but she cannot translate rapidly from one key to another. In fact, if we are playing a Bach prelude in the key of G and then move to another prelude in the key of B flat, she will falter even though she knows the second one very well.

There is another subtler problem with *June*: the second section does not fit logically with the first. If it were a single note, I would say it was sour. In and of itself, the second section is fine; however, there is no bridge or transitional passage to it. The key and tempo suddenly change, going from B flat to G and from andante to allegro, faster and faster, until the section ends as abruptly as it started in a series of glissandos. Given Tchaikovsky's fame for writing ballets such as *Swan Lake,* which he was working on at the same time as *The Seasons,* I would not be surprised if at this point in the composition he envisioned the ballerina retreating en point as the corp de ballet joyously springs on stage from the wings and then just as joyously rushes off.

Borrowing from the vocabulary of grammar, the syntax of the piece is off. The second section is like a dangling modifier, which reminds me of an apt example we were taught in seventh grade English class: "For sale a grand piano by an old lady with square legs." This is my personal opinion; other pianists may disagree. However, I am looking at it from the standpoint of internal logic coupled with the physical limits of a pianist who no longer has available to her the artifice of dazzling speed with which to cover up weaknesses in composition. Trina has an underlying musical syntactic sense that was not affected by the stroke. There is much debate among musical theoreticians about whether such a sense is innate or is learned (nature versus nurture). Certainly there is a large component of syntax that is culturally specific, hence learned. For example, the way the throat singers of Mongolia create sound, the gamelan music from Indonesia, and the 22 pitches of the Indian scale. For someone raised in the world of tonal music, it is nearly impossible to comprehend the patterns that are present therein. That said, there is still an underlying universal syntax or order that has to do with a planned, discernable arrangement of sound in time and the expectation of closure, i.e. that a piece has an integral beginning, middle and ending. Trina's sense of that order is intact. As a result, she instantly reacts when a note or passage in a piece of music is either syntactically off, dissonant, or seems to be. Sometimes when she plays a chord that sounds wrong, she will hesitate. "Yes?" she asks me urgently. About to be swamped by waves of oncoming notes, I shout back "Yes," adding frantically, "Don't stop! Keep going! It will resolve!" At the risk of mixing metaphors, that exhortation comically puts me in mind of standing on the deck of a storm-tossed ship shouting "steady as she goes!" to the helmsman as enormous waves sweep towards us.

All of this brings me back again to Johann Sebastian Bach and why Trina and I do so well with his music. His contrapuntal syntax is perfect. Even when his logic is beyond the reach of us poor middling pianists to fully grasp, we still sense it is there and find him trustworthy. His music is not inherently superior to that of, say, Beethoven or even Schoenberg. However, to Trina it is more comprehensible.

I should also add by way of confession that I never liked playing Bach when I was young for exactly the reasons I like playing him now. His piano music felt emotionally cold and controlled to me. Now Chopin—there was a composer who took risks! Some passages in his compositions give me the feeling of free-fall, with resolution billowing out like a parachute at the last heart-stopping moment. Not surprisingly, Trina and I struggle with all but Chopin's most elementary pieces. Had he been a writer and not a composer, Chopin would have intermixed very simple sentences with very complex ones, syntactically correct but a challenge to parse. In our case, Chopin is too much of a challenge, at least for now.

In playing with Trina, I am constantly aware of the analogy between music and language. Language has two entirely separate components: oral and written. So does music. A person can be musical yet be unable to read music, just as a person can be a good speaker yet be unable to read words. I know personally about the disjunction between speaking and reading because I come from a family of dyslexics who have a way with words verbally but who reverse letters, write down the wrong ones (e.g., *when* for *where, thought* for *through*), and are not aware of their mistakes. Similar to Trina's visual loss of the A note, we are blind to our errors, at least on first reading. We have laboriously trained ourselves to wait and then to reread what we have written, shifting manually from the internal point of view of the creator/writer to the external point of view of the editor/reader. Or failing in the task, we ask someone else to read what we have written before sending it into the world. (Stuck on my office wall is the following note from my son that he had attached to a letter: "Mom, could you proff this for me plese.")

For my son, learning to read was daunting. That he is now a good reader (though obviously not a good speller), I attribute to my reading to him beginning in infancy, implanting a love of books that gave him the willpower to overcome the immense challenges. Not surprisingly, his dyslexia also severely affected his ability to read music. My experience with Trina has served to deepen my appreciation of the complex sensuous web required to make music. The phrase to *sight-read,* meaning to play a piece for the first time, is apt, although it would be more accurate if it were *sight-read-hear-touch,* leaving out only taste and smell.

I finish playing *June* and place it on the empty bookcase next to the piano. Trina sits down beside me on the bench and opens a new piece that she has found in a box, the *Canon in D* by Pachelbel. "I don't know but we try," she says emphatically, one of her most repeated expressions, each word enunciated. A forerunner of Bach, Pachelbel also understood how to combine sound and sense. As Trina plays the slow bass, the physical disorder around us yields to the palliative order of sound. Even the poinsettia on the dining room table begins to look a little more secure.

UNRESOLVED CHORDS

Not being a musician, I would grade my piano skills as intermediate at best. Oddly, I consider my mediocrity to be a blessing because it means that I can never be mistaken for Trina's teacher. Instead, I play with her for pleasure as well as the grace of a friendship wherein communication is not reliant on language. Furthermore, before her stroke she was a better pianist than I. That is clear simply by looking at the music in her collection, well marked up and dog-eared from much playing.

There are empty spaces in my knowledge of Trina's musical past. I know she took piano lessons as a child and owned a spinet until about twelve years ago when she purchased the grand piano, her prized possession. About the same time, she began to take lessons again. Unfortunately, she cannot provide me with any details, resignedly repeating "I can't say." As to my speckled musical past, silence is probably the best course of action, yet I think some knowledge might help explain my relationship with Trina and my own love of music.

I was in second grade when I took my first piano lesson in a group class at my elementary school, a typical suburban brick edifice surrounded by asphalt with a tiny patch of trampled grass near the front entrance. While the steam banged and hissed in the radiators, we crowded together in a small, overheated basement room not much larger than a coat closet. Sitting meekly at wooden boards on which were painted the white and black notes, we were expected to practice scales as one child at a time took a turn at the real piano. I didn't last long. I was very shy, I thought the teacher was mean, and playing on a board held no appeal. So then, in a pattern that has remained with me my entire life, I began to teach myself on the big old upright in the corner of our living room, my feet not able to reach the pedals, eventually tackling *The Bells of St. Mary's* (the sheet music being in my mother's collection). It was far beyond my ability and the reach of my small hands, with its huge pounding chords mimicking the peal of the church bells, but I learned it anyway. How, I do not know, for I remember thinking that the little numbers written over the notes referred to the notes themselves instead of to the fingers that were to play the notes. To me, the number one referred not to the thumb but to middle C, number two not to the index finger but to middle D, etc. Eventually I realized my error, but when one teaches oneself, strange misunderstandings and peculiar ways of doing things often result.

While I did not have a piano teacher, I did have a piano mentor, none other than the illustrious Liberace (feathered, bejeweled and fabulous) whose show was on television every afternoon at 5:00. As I listened to him play, I danced around the room. I longed to take ballet lessons, but whereas my mother considered piano lessons to be acceptable with a modicum of usefulness (one could at least accompany hymn singing in Sunday school), she considered dancing lessons to be slightly effete and without one iota of practicality. I don't remember her ever saying these things outright, yet somehow that was the impression she gave me.

The other type of lesson I longed to take was accordion, which was very popular in the 1950s with door-to-door salesmen peddling package deals of an instrument and introductory lessons. I remember one salesman coming to our home and demonstrating the instrument, standing in the living room energetically playing a polka, tapping out the beat with his foot and swaying back and forth as he worked the bellows. I was enchanted with the little pearly buttons and the wide black strap, and wanted desperately for my mother to buy it. However, if ballet lessons were high class, accordion lessons were low class. I had no idea what polkas had to do with it, but I got the feeling from my mother's tone of voice that *real* music was not played on an accordion. Furthermore, there was simply no money in the family budget to buy another instrument, particularly when a perfectly good piano was standing in the living room.

When I restarted lessons in fifth grade, I hated them with the same vehemence that I had in second grade and stubbornly refused to practice except for a frantic hour right before each lesson. I was a trial to my staid piano teacher who had none of Liberace's flair or his amazing dimples. A friend of my mother's, she continued to teach me for two interminable years, more out of kindness than because she saw potential in me. Because my family could not afford to buy new music, I started with what my mother already owned that was not too difficult, which turned out to be the music of Grieg. His dark Nordic tonality, often in minor keys, sticks with me still. There was something magical about Grieg's music that so thoroughly evoked the frenzied dance of bloodthirsty trolls in the underground hall of the mountain king or the sprightly dance of elves. I never had a student book that set lessons in a pedagogical straight line, a book with sweet illustrations of bunny rabbits and children on swings. With Grieg, I jumped in whole, progressing rapidly to the sonatas of Clementi and Kuhlau. For that total immersion in real music, I have *not* always been thankful. Thankfulness for childhood things that required effort and discipline comes with age.

Although I quit playing piano, I never quit music,

learning to play guitar and singing in choirs. After my marriage, I acquired a second-hand Baldwin spinet, but it didn't get much use until one of my sons began to take lessons. When I started to play with Trina, I was coming back to an instrument that I had virtually abandoned. It is true that I have returned the piano to Trina, but it is equally true that she has returned the piano to me.

ONCE UPON A TIME

Fairy tales begin with the phrase "once upon a time" as if they take place in a world infinitely distant in a time beyond time, rather like a parallel universe both familiar and utterly strange. Once upon a time a woman named Trina played *Für Elise* by Ludwig Van Beethoven. Now another woman is attempting to play the treble with her left hand, reworking the fingering so that the arpeggios flow instead of trudge. Except there is no other woman—only Trina who knows exactly who she is, who totally rejects the duality of before and after, and who steadfastly refuses to wait for a happily-ever-after ending.

Playing melody does not come naturally to the left hand, which frequently must put up with the omp-pah-pah of rhythm. In fact, Chopin likened the left hand to a conductor keeping the beat. As a result, it can be heavy on the keys, having little experience with the quick delicacy of grace notes, the lightness of trills. Essentially, Trina's left hand needs to learn how to *sing* instead of to *accompany*. Because she played the piece before her stroke, Trina also needs to unlearn and relearn; that is the challenge that *Für Elise* presents her.

For me, the challenge is to overcome an unwarranted negativity toward *Für Elise*. I have heard it mangled many times by children who have memorized the notes without comprehending the entire piece, the result being a cloying repetition. Is there a demon crouching beneath the taut wires that summons a slightly precocious child to a vacant piano bench to pound out *Für Elise*? I think that there is. I also think the demon of banality must be driven out because the piece deserves better. To help accomplish that, I have brought with me today a rendition by Van Cliburn on compact disk to which we begin to listen. Simple and pure, it is redemptive.

Beethoven wrote *Für Elise* for Therese Malfatti, his doctor's 18-year-old daughter. Not much is known about her, although there is some speculation he may have been in love with her, that she was in fact his "Immortal Beloved" about whom he wrote longingly. The title is not really a title but a dedication: *for Therese*, which was apparently misread by a publisher as Elise. All we know for certain is that she was the recipient of a small piece of music that is quintessentially Beethoven, particularly in the 59th through the 76th measures, when the bass begins to drive on the A note below low C, not loud, not pounding, but passionately persistent. If the passage is played too heavily it becomes melodramatic, but if played as if the heartbeat has suddenly quickened, it imparts an inner urgency that is quite powerful. *Für Elise* is nothing less than a love letter in notes, written after the Sixth Symphony and before the Seventh, when Beethoven was forty years old and already going deaf. After all, a love letter is merely a written communication of desire. And did not Beethoven achieve that in *Für Elise*?

When Van Cliburn reaches the end of the piece, I turn off the music and we sit in silence. Finally Trina says "yesterday." Knowing what she means, I say "four years." Nothing else is said. Additional words are unnecessary and, in fact, would diminish the enormity of what has just been communicated. Yesterday was the anniversary of her stroke, leading to her life being turned upside down. But it also led to *this* place, to *this* now, and to the playing of a song that Beethoven wrote alone at a piano, facing a future without the ability to hear and uncertain whether the love he felt would be returned.

Fourteen years later in 1824, never having married his Elise, Beethoven directed the first performance of the *Ninth Symphony*. By then he had gone totally deaf. When it ended, he stood facing the orchestra and the chorus with his back to the audience, unaware of the thundering roar behind him until someone turned him around. I can envision him looking out on that throng of faces, mouths shaping the silent word bravo, hands making the motion of clapping, while the only thing he could hear was the pizzicato of his own heartbeat.

When emotions are easily manipulated, whether by story or music, the result is sentimentality: a shallow sense of loss to be enjoyed, not acted upon; tragedy stripped of grief. The story about Beethoven conducting the *Ninth* is often told, yet when I hear it I also hear in my mind the magnificent chorale finale *Ode to Joy*, which guts it of sentimentality.

Yesterday, four years ago, once upon a time. Those words cannot be banished forever, but their power to pull down and hold back can be drained from them. All it takes is for Trina and me to sit down at the piano and begin to play *Für Elise* once upon *this* time.

THE MIND GAME

Sound is heard by the ear but music is constructed by the mind. The major difference between a string of single notes and a piece of music is the listener's perception of a time connection between the notes. If I play *Für Elise* a note a minute, in 779 minutes I will have reached the final A chord, but the most patient of listeners would probably not have discerned that I played music. The listener would have thought that once each minute I strolled into the living room and hit a random note, then left again to fold a towel or pour milk into my cup of coffee before returning to hit another note. In 12 hours and 59 minutes, he would have become totally convinced of my oddity but not of my musicality. By absurdly stretching out the playing of the piece, I would have deprived him of the ability to make connections between the notes, thereby comprehending patterns of repetition and variation.

Why is a theme (played in a normal span of time) identifiable when it is reintroduced several minutes later, this time in a minor key with a different rhythm? Because if the listener has been paying attention, she will have learned the theme sufficiently to be aware of its modification. In fact, the ability to perceive theme and variation is an essential component of the mind game, maintaining the listener's interest. With *Für Elise*, the game is easy because of the frequent repetitions of the theme. It is easy as well with Pachelbel's *Canon* and Couperin's *Rondo* that Trina and I have played. With other pieces, the game is far more difficult. Fortunately, knowing a piece well doesn't end the game because good music is meant to be heard and reheard. In fact, one indication of artistic greatness is that familiarity does not breed contempt. A superb work has the powerful capacity to remain new.

In his book *Music and Humanism: An Essay in the Aesthetics of Music*, R. A. Sharpe writes about the important roles that repetition and memorability play in enhancing the desire to hear a piece again: "I do not drive to work with the catchy melodies of Schoenberg, Boulez, or Berg running through my head, as the music of Britten or Shostakovich might." Sharpe concludes that he is not haunted by the music of the first three. His use of the word *haunted* is appropriate, as if a humming ghost had taken up residence in his mind. My own humming ghost tends to get stuck on melodies such as Gershwin's *Fascinating Rhythm* to the point that I am in dire need of a good exorcist.

Another essential component of the mind game is mental anticipation, which is a kind of *pre-thinking*. Puns and jokes are obvious examples: the mind pre-thinks a split second before someone utters the next word in a sentence. If the word is unanticipated, laughter may be the mind's reaction to being caught pleasantly in its own error. For instance, in the comic Rodney Dangerfield's signature line "Take my wife, please," you expect him to say the words "for example." The unexpected use of "please" turns the first three words into a command that is also a supplication. However, in situations not involving comedians, if your mind is caught unpleasantly in its error, your reaction will range from benign befuddlement to dismay, even outrage.

Another example of mental anticipation is if you take a sip from what you think is a glass of water only to sputter in surprise at finding it to be vodka. Had you anticipated vodka, there would have been no such reaction. The same is true with music; your brain anticipates a certain note to be played next. When it occurs, you experience a feeling of pleasure. But when your brain is too successful at anticipating, you become bored. Hopefully at that point, you hear something unexpected and original and your interest is renewed. It is all part of the mind game.

Mental anticipation goes far beyond syntax and what the listener has learned about structure and Western musical style. Predictive, it permeates all physical action as in the example of sipping the glass of water cum vodka. Despite her stroke, when Trina plays the first E followed by D sharp of *Für Elise*, she has already pre-thought the 3/8th time, the absence of sharps and flats in the signature, the pianissimo, the alignment of her arm, and the placement of the fingers (rearranged for the left hand), beginning with the thumb, followed by the second finger. She will, a nanosecond before it is required, prepare for the crescendo on the third note and the decrescendo on the sixth and will have determined what that means in terms of finger pressure on the keys in readiness for my entry in the bass on the ninth note. It has been frequently pointed out that only humans have music, the reason being that it requires a high level of intelligence to discern and remember sound patterns. While I am not sure I agree—having listened to a lone mocking bird in the middle of the night improvise for the sheer fun of it—I cannot deny that music requires intelligence.

Trina and I bring to bear a host of physical and mental skills when we practice *Für Elise*. Eyes scan left to right and up and down, skipping between the staves to read the bass and treble, then doubling back to the beginning of the next line. Fingers coordinate in rhythm to such a high degree it is hard to name an activity more demanding of the human hands. The foot depresses and releases the pedals as indicated by markings on the music. And those are just some of the kinetic skills. While it is generally true that a predominance of language skills reside in the left hemisphere and music skills in the right, recent scientific studies have shown that music perception is split among many neural networks all over the brain. Neurobiologists can identify different sections of the brain and, by means of scans and physiological and psychological tests, begin to determine what each one does, but even if they are broadly correct, they will not be close to what those areas do in totality. The technology is too imprecise, too focused on recording the mountain peaks of cellular energy without fully considering the significance of the hills and valleys of that energy or the vast web of channels and rivers ebbing and flowing between them.

The non-locality of musical perception and ability helps explain why shortly after her stroke Trina could recite Robert Frost's poem *Stopping By the Woods* with me and could sing folk songs as we played the autoharp. Language is principally a left-brain skill, but when words are linked to music or are in the form of poetry with rhythm and rhyme, it is the right brain that finds room for them. Non-locality also explains why Trina plays piano as well as she does. Additionally, it is fortunate that she studied so much music before the stroke because stored memory, even though imperfect, provides the equivalent of trail marks. Due to her prior knowledge of the aural pathway mapped by Beethoven, she can now move from the beginning to the end of *Für Elise*, with only a slight rerouting required.

However, a few weeks ago Trina began to play a new piece: Moritz Moszkowski's *Etude, Op. 92, #4* for the left hand. It is the first major work she has played solo since her stroke. Moszkowski (1854-1925) was a concert pianist, composer and teacher. He probably wrote the series of twelve etudes to strengthen the left hands of his students, two of whom were to achieve musical fame: the English conductor Thomas Beecham and the pianist and harpsichordist Wanda Landowska. *Etude #4* is a flowing series of arpeggios with enough repetition to satisfy the part of the brain that craves the serenity of the expected and enough interesting chord progressions to satisfy that part of the brain that craves the excitement of the unexpected.

My first job is to sit as far to the right on the piano bench as is possible and not fall off, thereby allowing Trina to slide sideways to reach the upper end of the keyboard. My second job is to encourage her not to give up because playing this piece is difficult and tires her out. And my third job is to remind her when necessary to play F sharp instead of F natural because the piece is written in the key of G. Like the A, the F sharp occasionally goes absent without leave. My quiet cue must be given just as her fingers move over the keyboard toward the F so that the flow is not broken. It underscores the mental complexity of playing the piano. It underscores as well how enormous an accomplishment it will be when Trina reaches the end of *Etude #4*.

"I DIED FOR BEAUTY"

Beginning in the sixteenth century, choirboys with perfect pitch were sometimes castrated so that their voices would not drop during puberty. While publicly condemning the practice, privately the Catholic Church encouraged it. As a result, thousands of boys, mostly from poor families, went under the knife. By all accounts, the adult sopranos thus manufactured had the high, pure voices of boys with the lung capacity of men. It also resulted in humans who could never live normal lives and who were denied freedom of choice by people who thought the beauty of songs was worth more than the well-being of singers. When the Italian castrato Farinelli sang evening after evening to King Philip of Spain to relieve his severe melancholia, was his music evil? Certainly not, but the technique used to achieve it was. By many accounts, the castrato voice was the most beautiful of all human sounds. May such terrible beauty never exist again.

Recently I began to talk about piano lessons with a friend. Suddenly his face became contorted with anger. He told me that as a child he had taken lessons from a nun who had cruelly beaten him whenever he hit a wrong note. Under pressure from his parents, he endured her brutality for two long years before he quit and never went back. This man loves music, yet I could see in his eyes that the pain was still present as he recalled being hit on the side of the head.

In both these examples, a child's well-being was sacrificed to the beauty of the music. Whenever the worth of a person is set lower than the worth of what is created, the result is inhumane, an all too frequent occurrence not just in the arts but in sports. The recent history of drug use by young athletes to achieve short-term enhancement of performance at the cost of their long-term health is parallel to the castration of young male singers. Ethically we have not progressed as far from the sixteenth century as we would like to think.

In Emily Dickinson's poem "I died for Beauty," truth and beauty lie in adjoining graves talking softly back and forth about why they failed. I think Dickinson meant that the two "Kinsmen" should never have been separated and that philosophical discussion, despite being carried on for eons, is worthless, which she expressed metaphorically as moss reaching their lips and covering up their names. Farinelli and my friend did not die for beauty; they were maimed for it. Too young to protect themselves from the actions of adults who were supposed to help them, they were also maimed for truth.

In this series of reflections on music and the mind, why would I choose to include one on cruelty? The reason is that if these reflections became more important to me than Trina herself, she could be badly hurt. Against her will, she would be turned into a subject manipulated by me for the sake of an unseen audience of readers. To avoid this, I have given her each essay as it neared completion, and I have asked her permission to share them with other people, even to submit them for publication. One day I gave a selection to a friend who is in the field of publishing, and mentioned it to Trina while we were sitting together on the piano bench. She asked me why. This was not a casual *why*. This *why* was like the wail of a child about to be sent away from home forever, or of a person betrayed by a close friend. It cut through me, making absurd any appeal on my part to the healing power of the word. I resolved right then that if the reflections hurt her, they would have to end and I would have to accept their destruction as right and good. Yet Trina also knew that the *why* was directed at herself and at God. Why did the stroke happen? Why play piano? Why go on living? And her answer that day and every week since has been to play and to try, pushing back against beatific and untruthful acceptance, and to encourage me to continue writing and sharing.

STONY LONESOME

In her book *Harmonies of Heaven and Earth: The Spiritual Dimension of Music from Antiquity to the Avant-Garde*, Joscelyn Godwin relates a story about a Trappist abbey in America. Trappists take a life-long vow of silence, but that does not preclude singing that uplifts them spiritually and helps to give flow to their days, beginning at dawn with matins and ending with soothing complin in the evening before they retire for the night. That changed following Vatican II in 1958, when the abbey complied with the directive to cease singing in Latin, which meant an end to Gregorian chant. Things immediately began to go wrong. First the monks became tired, finding that four or five hours of sleep a night were no longer sufficient. Sickness and psychological problems increased. According to Godwin, "After trying various conventional remedies, all unsuccessfully, they began to wonder whether the cause of their ills might be the loss of the hours they used to devote to singing the liturgy in Gregorian chant. So with special dispensation they went back to their old routine, and their troubles gradually disappeared."

From the standpoint of faith, some people might contend that the silent prayers of the monks should have been sufficient communication, but they weren't. Others might surmise that there was a mysterious quality to the Gregorian chant essential to the monks' spiritual well-being. But the human need that went unmet once the singing stopped was basic: They longed to hear their own individual voices chanting aloud, joining with other voices as part of a community of shared understanding. Music helped them to balance their separateness as well as maintain their peace of mind. The same is true for Trina.

There is a place along the Hudson River near West Point called Stony Lonesome. I don't know where the name came from, but it has always conveyed to me the cold, hard, unyielding state of being cut off from others, unable to speak one's thoughts. Aphasia is a synonym for Stony Lonesome. Certainly Trina can *listen* to music, just as the monks could listen to scripture, but listening breaks neither silence nor solitude. It is a solipsistic activity in which the person takes in but does not give out. To sing, or in our case to play music together, breaks through silence and solitude.

Every so often when we finish playing a piece, Trina will lean her head against my shoulder for a brief second, her way of saying all at once, "that was lovely," "thanks," and "see you tomorrow." Perhaps at a certain level Gregorian chant can be translated the same way. And so I hope that this evening somewhere in the heartland of America, Trappist monks are singing and that after the music ends, they silently lean their heads ever so slightly in each other's direction as if to say "that was lovely," "thanks" and "see you tomorrow."

THE MOONFLOWER

We have just finished playing Massenet's *Elegy*. In the kitchen, our loyal audience of one—Mick—is chopping the ingredients for stew. Two piles of carrots and celery are growing taller beside the cutting board. After Trina's stroke, Mick retired from his full-time job and started a handyman business that gave him more freedom to take her to numerous medical and therapy appointments. He also took on the responsibility of cooking. Fortunately, he is good at it, as the enticing aroma of braising beef, herbs and onions attests. I have made myself a cup of hibiscus tea that I have set on the bookshelf next to the piano, but I am a little hungry. A bowl of stew would be nice.

Before I head home, Trina and I sit down in the dining room so I can finish my tea. On the table is an illustrated library book *The Trellis and the Seed* by Jan Karon that she is reading with the help of a friend who comes twice a week. Trina likes the book so much she starts to read it to me. The story is rather like Hans Christian Anderson's *The Ugly Ducking* rewritten for gardeners. The main character is not a baby swan but a moonflower that is slow to germinate and grow. As the other flowers in the garden spurt upward and blossom, the moonflower gets discouraged because it is still all leaf and vine. Then one evening late in the summer it blooms, and its sweet scent floats on the night breeze.

Trina makes it through two pages, arduously sounding out every single word. Even when a word appears several times on the page, she will nevertheless sound it out all over again. Little words such as "the," "if," and "when" are particularly difficult. The problem is that, unlike the moonflower seed that takes root in the soil, the words do not easily take root in her brain. Each time she reads a word, it is new.

What is illuminating is that there are two levels of reading (or cognition) going on. For example, she comes to the word *climb* (the moonflower climbs up a trellis) and can't read it; instead she says without hesitation the word *hike*. When I tell her that is incorrect, she arduously sounds out *climb,* running through the alphabet to determine the first letter (not too far for c), and then taking the word apart phonetically. However, it is apparent that when her eyes first fell on the word *climb* and sent on the information via a trail of neurons, part of her brain comprehended the word even though it was unable to transmit it (via yet another trail of neurons) to the part of the brain responsible for reading orally. Stymied, the brain adroitly substituted the synonym *hike.* This happens frequently: *building* for *house, ocean* for *sea, flower* for *rose.* One of Trina's oft-repeated phrases is "I know but I can't say." And, indeed, she does know, and, indeed, she can't say, at least not easily.

Semantics has to do with meaning while syntax has to do with grammar. Stroke can hit one or both. When my mother had her first stroke and suffered aphasia, the result was very different than what occurred with Trina. Meaning became scrambled so that she would say nonsensical strings of words that were, despite their craziness, identifiable as sentences. It was as if she had stumbled into the domain of Lewis Carroll's *Jabberwocky* and was lisping, "'Twas brillig, and the slithy toves/ Did gyre and gimble in the wabe." My mother's stroke affected the Wernicke's area of her brain and is, therefore, called Wernicke's aphasia (named for the German physician

Carl Wernicke). Trina has what is called Broca's area aphasia (named for the French physician Pierre Paul Broca) in which the brain knows the meaning of words but can't say them, let alone put them together into grammatical sentences. This is why she has difficulty reading conjunctions and prepositions such as *for, with* or the definite article *the.* These words have no inherent meaning. Their sole purpose is syntactic: to connect and show relationships between various parts of speech, such as nouns, verbs, adjectives and adverbs. However, her ability to determine meaning and meaninglessness points to a deep neural tie between syntax and semantics; they are reliant on each other.

These difficulties carry over into Trina's reading of music notation. If I point to a note on the music and ask her to tell me what it is called, for example G natural, she will try to find the answer by starting physically at the A note on the keyboard and working up from there. It is parallel to her working through the alphabet to identify the first letter of a word. However, she often has difficulty finding the A. Yet, if I ask her to play the G natural without saying it, she will invariably get it right. So also if I ask her to say aloud the name of a sharp or flat in the key signature, she will guess, usually wrong. Yet if I ask her to play it, she will do so without error. Her fingers are "speaking" correctly, similar to the way in which her brain comprehended *climb* but could not vocalize it.

The problem the moonflower had was that its entire manner of being differed from the flowers around it: they bloomed early, it bloomed late; they bloomed during the day, it bloomed at night; their beauty was in their color, its beauty was in its scent. No wonder Trina likes the story of the moonflower: At night, in its own time, it blooms.

RAPTURE OF THE DEEP

On a late March day leaning toward spring, we listen to Leon Fleisher play Ravel's *Concerto in D Major for the Left Hand.* It was recorded in 1990 with the Boston Symphony Orchestra under the direction of Seiji Ozawa, before Fleisher recovered the full use of his right hand. The concerto is outrageously difficult, yet so exquisitely full is the sound, it seems as if Fleisher is playing with two hands. His performance is as effortless as the thickening of rose-hued maple buds and the strengthening of the sunlight; as forceful as the upwelling of sap from cold roots and the surge of rivers suddenly freed of ice. Never having heard left-hand music played before, Trina is astonished at how beautiful it is. She is also exhilarated, because this is not a disabled man playing music that at its best reminds the listener of what is lacking. On the contrary, it is lush and sustaining, brought to fruition by the efforts of three people: Wittgenstein who commissioned it; Fleisher; and Ravel who at the time he composed the concerto did not know that brain damage would make it one of his last.

Ravel subtitled the concerto *Mixed Muses*, indicating its range of styles. In their behavior, the Greek muses, who were responsible for the arts and sciences, could either be radiantly good or horribly bad, as peaceful as a fountain or as destructive as a tsunami. And the concerto is indeed both peaceful and martial, with an introspective andante and a strident march, sardonically undercut by a jazz rhythm on the piano. At one point, side drums echo Ravel's famous piece *Bolero*.

The concerto begins so low in the auditory range (with basses and double bassoons) that at first it is more felt than heard, like a tremor. Somber and slow, it could be considered evocative of war and onrushing darkness, as some of Ravel's contemporaries interpreted it. However, to me it evokes the song of a whale as it rises from the deep, finally breaching the surface of a sun-sparkled sea, expressed in the music as a D major chord blasted by the brass. Then the orchestra is silenced as the piano comes in alone, echoing what has just been played, starting with the lowest sounds the keyboard can produce and ascending to the highest. If the orchestra is whale-like, then the piano is dolphin-like—sleeker, more playful, as fond of the sky as of the sea. Both creatures are capable of breaching the surface, but the first gleefully smashes back down while the second slips in with barely a ripple.

In his biography of Ravel, Gerald Lerner writes that the mis-impression of the piece being evocative of doom has to do with the deep bass being the natural range of the left hand. "So that the piano would not seem freakish in this respect, Ravel had to favor the lower registers of the orchestra. It is for that rather than any sinister reason that the first theme arises from the shadowy nether regions, on double bassoon against quietly rumbling cellos and basses."

Lower register or not, the plangent andante gives me a chill. The *rapture of the deep* is the term used to describe the bends, a warped mental state of euphoria brought on by oxygen deprivation and the build up of nitrogen in the bloodstream. Perhaps that is what is happening to me because by the end of the piece, I need to decompress. It is not just the beauty of the music itself that affects me so strongly but what I know about the composer, the pianist, the man who commissioned the piece, and Trina—all coming together this afternoon.

Ravel began developing neurological problems in the late 1920s, but they were not debilitating. Then in October 1932 he was in an automobile accident in Paris. He suffered a concussion that led to the onset of both aphasia and ataxia (the inability to write). While he managed to compose a few songs following the crash, he found to his enormous frustration that he could no longer write down the music he was composing in his head. So the *Concerto for the Left Hand* is one of Ravel's last major works, along with the *Piano Concerto in G Major* written in the same period. Ravel lived for five more years, finally dying in 1937 after undergoing a surgical procedure in hopes of alleviating his condition. Not long before his death, he attended a concert of his piece *Daphnis and Chloë*. "It is beautiful. It is beautiful after all," he declared, then added plaintively, "I leave nothing. I have not said what I wanted to say. I have so much more to say." But Ravel was wrong. Perhaps he did not say all he wanted to say, yet today in his *Concerto for the Left Hand*, he spoke to us about how piano music is not diminished by being played with only one hand. And it was beautiful, beautiful after all.

INSIDE THE PIANO

Yesterday I dusted Trina's piano inside and out which gave me the opportunity to study its workings as I attempted to expel the gray bane of fastidious people. As is true of most instruments, the piano is beautiful, although from an acoustic standpoint beauty is not a necessity. Outside: the striking contrast of ivory and ebony keys. Inside: the diagonal slash of gleaming steel and copper wires wrapped around hitch and tuning pins attached to a stalwart iron frame, each pin stoically withstanding approximately 1000 Newtons of force. Little red felt hammers wait in readiness to strike upwards against the wires, sending waves through the spruce soundboard. Around everything curves the polished wood case shaped rather like a lyre resting on its side. The lyre was sacred to Apollo who in Greek mythology was both the first virtuoso and the first music teacher. Since Apollo was also the god of rationality and order, it occurred to me that if he had an avatar it was probably Bach playing the piano.

This particular piano was built by the Hallet and Davis Piano Company in 1917, around the time when the piano industry went into a steep and permanent decline brought on by the inventions of the automobile, record player and radio. The first claimed a fair chunk of a middle class family's income, and the other two fulfilled their desire for music in a way that was instant and simple. Why bother with the work and expense of playing the piano when music could flow into a home with a turn of a knob?

As I dusted, Trina tried to explain to me a new therapy apparatus she hopes will return motion to her clenched right hand. I am not sure how it works but apparently it has gears and springs that somehow attach to the back of her fingers and from there to her forearm so that when she closes her fist, which she is able to do slightly, the apparatus will reopen the fingers, thereby working the muscles. I presume that the goal is to reestablish neural networks, working from the outposts (the fingers) back to the heart of the kingdom (the brain). Leery, I wonder how many messages the fingers must send before a faint message is returned. Nevertheless, it is good to see Trina so excited about trying a new approach. Most people who have had strokes reach a point where progress stops, but Trina is still improving, each day struggling to solve the conundrum of what is known as the serenity prayer: "God grant me the serenity to accept the things I cannot change, courage to change the things I can, and wisdom to know the difference." There was a tiny quiver in the wires as my dust cloth swept over them one last time.

And now I shall briefly set aside the topics of dust, beauty, mythology, the decline of the piano industry, physical therapy, and prayer in preparation for an attempt to take them all up again in a new, hopefully insightful, way. Bear with me. A few weeks ago I succumbed to the allure of a sales catalog of remaindered books from academic presses. The book that tipped the balance in my decision to buy was one on linguistics. It was inexpensive and would fill a major gap in my library. Of course, I then ordered several more books so it would not be lonely during shipping: the poetry of Pablo Neruda; a text on modern Hebrew; the Cambridge *Companion to the Piano*; and Rilke's *Sonnets to Orpheus* translated by David Young. They arrived two days ago.

Each morning before I get out of bed, I read whatever book is nearest at hand as I drink my first cup of coffee brought to me by my considerate husband. Yesterday morning before breakfast, I read the entire *Companion to the Piano,* and today at 5:45 a.m., I opened Rilke's *Sonnets to Orpheus* and got as far as Number 3:

A god can do it. But tell me how
a man can follow him through the narrow
lyre. The human self is split; where two
heartways cross, there is no temple to Apollo.

Song, as you teach it, is not desire, not
a wooing of something that's finally attained;
song is existence. Easy for the god. But
when do we exist? And when does he spend

the earth and the stars on our being?
When we love? That's what you think when you're young;
not so, though your voice forces open your mouth, —

learn to forget how you sang. That fades.
Real singing is a different kind of breath.
A nothing-breath. A ripple in the god. A wind.

That I am now up and out of bed and am writing down these thoughts is proof that a human being can experience the onslaught of awe and live to tell about it.

I do not know if Rilke read Hebrew, although perhaps he knew some individual words. I know he respected Martin Buber, the Jewish scholar whose work *Daniel* influenced the writing of Rilke's seminal *The Duino Elegies.* I suspect that he at least knew the Hebrew word *ruach,* meaning *wind, spirit, soul,* and *breath.* It was *ruach* that brooded over the waters of chaos at the moment of creation in Genesis. And it is *ruach* that broods over the keys of a thoroughly dusted piano as Trina and I find our way through the wires—each wire under enormous tension just to be able to sound one single note.

Yet the myth of Orpheus is also cautionary. His musical skill is so great he can charm nature. As soon as he sets his fingers to the strings of his lyre, predators lie down with prey in a peaceable musical kingdom. When in his absence, his beloved Eurydice dies of snakebite shortly after their wedding, Orpheus considers himself equal to the task of charming death to bring her back from the underworld, and he nearly succeeds. It is his joy at seeing the sun as they climb single-file toward the light that is their undoing. He turns to Eurydice, as Hades had warned him not to, and she disappears forever. Is the failure caused by the hubris of Orpheus in thinking himself capable of overcoming death by his skill? Is it caused by his impetuosity in turning around too early? Or is the reason his overestimation of the power of music? Most likely it is all three. Even if it *were* possible, it is not for Orpheus to bring Eurydice back, just as it is not for me to bring Trina back. Orpheus's attempt reveals that he misunderstands the nature of music, which is not to restore but simply to *be*.

And so it is that in the afternoons, two friends—sisters now—play music, building a temple out of sound and silence where their heartways cross. And therein, between the serenity to accept and the courage to change, they seek for the wisdom to know the difference.

POSTLUDE

Unfortunately, the intense physical therapy with a mechanical device attached to Trina's right hand did not bring about any improvement. The device could not be adjusted properly for the position of her fingers. Furthermore, the grueling daily exercises often left her too exhausted to play piano, practice reading, and enjoy the company of her family. After a year, she returned to more traditional therapy.

Perhaps in the future there will be a medical breakthrough that will fully restore Trina's abilities. Until then, we will continue to play piano together.

SELECTED BIBLIOGRAPHY

Damasio, Antonio, R. *The Feeling of What Happens: Body and Emotion in the Making of Consciousness.* Harcourt Brace & Co., 1999.

—*Looking for Spinoza: Joy, Sorrow and the Feeling Brain.* Harcourt, Inc., 2003.

Evenson, Brad. "We Just Can't Get that Song out of Our Heads." National Post, 2003.
http://www.flatrock.org.nz/wolf/wolf_den/music/why_we_can't-forget_songs.htm

Godwin, Joscelyn. *Harmonies of Heaven and Earth: The Spiritual Dimension of Music from Antiquity to the Avant-Garde.* Rochester, Vermont: Inner Traditions International, Inc., 1987, pgs. 63-64.

James, Burnett. *Ravel: His Life and Times.* New York: Midas Books, Hippocrene Books, 1983.

Jourdain, Robert. *Music, the Brain and Ecstasy: How Music Captures Our Imagination.* New York: William Morrow and Company, Inc., 1997, pgs. 60, 331.

Karon, Jan. *The Trellis and the Seed.* New York: Viking Books, 2003.

Kivy, Peter. *The Corded Shell: Reflections on Musical Expression.* Princeton, NJ: Princeton University Press, 1980.

Larner, Gerald. *Maurice Ravel.* London: Phaidon Press Limited, 1996.

Malcolm, Norman. *Ludwig Wittgenstein: A Memoir.* London: Oxford University Press, 1958.

Rilke, Rainer Maria. *Sonnets to Orpheus.* Trans. David Young. New Hampshire: Wesleyan University Press and University Press of New England, 1987.

Rosen, Charles. *The Frontiers of Meaning: Three Informal Lectures on Music.* New York: Hill and Wang, 1994.

Rowland, David, ed. *The Cambridge Companion to the Piano.* Cambridge: Cambridge University Press, 1998.

Sacks, Oliver, *Awakenings.* New York: Simon & Schuster, 1987, pg. 60.
—*The Man Who Mistook His Wife for a Hat and Other Clinical Tales.* New York: Simon & Schuster Inc., 1970. Touchstone Edition, 1998.
—*Musicophilia.* New York: Vintage Books, 2008.

Scruton, Roger. *The Aesthetics of Music.* Oxford, England: Clarendon Press, 1997.

Serafine, Mary Louise. *Music as Cognition: The Development of Thought in Sound.* New York: Columbia University Press, 1988.

Sharpe. R. A. *Music and Humanism: An Essay in the Aesthetics of Music.* Oxford England: Oxford University Press, 2000, pg. 196.

Sloboda, John A. *The Musical Mind: The Cognitive Psychology of Music.* Oxford, England: Clarendon Press, 1985.

Storr, Anthony. *Music and the Mind.* New York: The Free Press, 1992.

Wittgenstein, Ludwig. *Philosophical Investigations.* New York: The Macmillan Co., 1958, pg. 143.

PERMISSIONS

ACKNOWLEDGEMENTS

A special thanks to Michelle Housley, my talented daughter-in-law, for her thoughtful editing. Also thanks to Mick Groshart for his constancy and encouragement.

Author photo by Tara Doyle.

ABOUT THE AUTHOR

Kathleen L. Housley is an independent researcher, writer and poet who has written for numerous journals, including *Image, The Christian Century,* and the *Global Spiral* (online). In *Firmament* (Higganum Hill Books 2007), she explores through poetry the borderlands between science and religion, the physical and the spiritual. This type of interdisciplinary exploration also occurs in *Keys to the Kingdom: Reflections on Music and the Mind* wherein she brings together neurology and music. She is also a volunteer emergency medical technician—an avocation that has provided her a unique perspective on the nature of health and wholeness.

Housley is the author of three biographies of unusual women: *The Letter Kills But the Spirit Gives Life, The Smiths* (Historical Society of Glastonbury 1993); *Emily Hall Tremaine: Collector on the Cusp* (University Press of New England 2001); and *Tranquil Power: The Art and Life of Perle Fine* (MidMarch Arts Press 2005).

Breinigsville, PA USA
21 November 2010
249745BV00001B/2/P